Guide to Social Engineering

Guide to Social Engineering

A Beginner's Guide for the Novice

Dauda Sule

Guide to Social Engineering

A Beginner's Guide for the Novice

Dauda Sule

Table of contents

INTRODUCTION

Cyber crime, cyber espionage, cyber terrorism, cyber warfare! In recent times society has become more and more dependent on electronic devices and platforms. This is a result of technological advancements that have gone a long way in making life easier for everyone; but unfortunately it has also made life easier for the bad guys who use the technology to cause havoc, whether through breaches, theft destruction and so on. Hence, there is a need for us as individuals, organizations or nation states to ensure that our information and data are safe and secure on these electronic devices and platforms before using, while using and after using them. Whether the devices are computers, tablets, mobile phones, medical devices, or platforms like networks (the Internet, corporate networks, mobile networks, etc), social media networks, apps, games and so on; they are all vulnerable to threats which we need to protect against; and that also includes data and information that is on them and passes through them – hence cyber security.

For cyber security to be efficient and effective there is a need to have an understanding of how malicious actors carry out their activities to be able to plan for and mitigate against their attacks and breaches. In cyber security circles it is said that you should not plan thinking if you will be hit a negative cyber incident, but should think in terms of when you will be hit (and nowadays it is becoming more like when you discover you have been hit). A trending method used by malicious actors is social engineering. Social engineering saves these perpetrators a lot of trouble making it easy for them to compromise individuals, compromising individuals could be the end or the means to an end. The individual could be the target; it could be the organization where the individual works or society he/she belongs to – the individual's compromise can be used to get at the organization or society.

This book seeks to provide a simple guide to individuals to protect themselves in this day and age from current threats to their personal security and/or the security of where they work or belong. The book is targeted at those who don't have advanced understanding of IT and cyber security and are not very IT savvy. The phenomenon of social engineering as it affects cyber security is presented in a simple manner with examples to aid in not just improving personal cyber safety and security but also getting a better understanding and appreciation of cyber security and its importance

CYBER SECURITY AND SOCIAL ENGINEERING

WHAT IS CYBER SECURITY?

Securing electronic devices and platforms from potential and existing threats, amounts to cyber security. Rouse (2016) defined cyber security as the combination of technology, processes and practices designed to protect networks, computers, programs and data from attack, damage or unauthorized access. The definition highlights what was mentioned in the introduction (that is the devices and platforms; and the data and information on and passing through them) and how to get them secured from threats. The threats could be from external attackers, malicious insiders, or unintentional threats arising from negligence or accidents.

There can also be some issues that could arise which are legal or regulatory in nature - like compliance with regulatory issues in respect of data management and protection, litigation requiring evidence that is digital in nature to be readily and credibly available. These issues have an impact or are impacted by how information and data are managed and secured. For example, the Payment Card Industry Data Security Standard (PCI DSS), the EU General Data Protection Regulation (GDPR), and so on, have correlation with cyber security.

Measures can be put in place to protect information and information systems which include use of hardware and software, like firewalls, antivirus programs, intrusion detection systems (IDS) and intrusion protection systems (IPS). Cyber security is not restricted to only securing hardware and software, devices and platforms; it also involves ensuring the physical environment in which the aforementioned are located, and the users and operators, are all secure. Physical security needs to be established to restrict those who have access to information systems in order to protect the systems and also ensure accountability – where malicious individuals can have physical access to information systems; they can easily steal information/data or hardware, install malicious software, damage or destroy the information systems, irrespective of any security hardware/software in place.

The users of information systems and the operators are crucial for ensuring cyber security. Humans are the weakest link as far as cyber security is concerned, and you as secure as your weakest link. Human beings can be easily deceived into releasing sensitive information and data, like usernames and passwords; they can be made to shut down security systems giving malicious individuals unfettered access; they can be manipulated to install malware; and so on. Special care has to be given to the human factor, because no matter the technology deployed to protect information systems; those that operate the system make or break the protection.

Malicious actors can have various motives for carrying out their cyber attacks; to steal from individuals and organizations, could be political, some form of activism, warfare and so on – the attacks could be for cyber crime, cyber espionage, cyber terrorism or cyber warfare. Criminal use information technology to compromise victims, this is referred to as cyber crime. Cyber espionage could be carried out by organizations or nation states – business organizations may steal information from their competitors in order to get an edge; nation states spy on adversarial nation states for defensive and offensive purposes. Terrorist organizations also use technology to wreak havoc through cyber terrorism; they could target crucial industries or infrastructure to destabilize their victims. Some activists also indulge in some form of hacking to press their point, like environmental and social activists. Notable is the hacker organization "Anonymous" which has been known to target victims like organizations or nation states as a form of protest against actions it dislikes. Nation states can engage in cyber warfare by targeting critical infrastructure; for example Russia was accused of targeting the Ukrain's government, banks and power grid in 2015 during the dispute between the two countries.

The actions could be targeted directly at information systems to compromise, damage or destroy; could be to retrieve sensitive and confidential data; or could use the information systems as a stepping stone to wreak social havoc by spreading propaganda and fake news, or damage infrastructure – civilian or military. The malicious entities usually hit their targets by first getting access to the information systems then proceed from there. The easiest way to get the access is compromising individuals. Personally identifiable information (PII) like usernames, passwords, date of birth and other demographic information can be retrieved from individuals through deceit in order to compromise the individuals, their organization or their society; and this can be achieved by way of social engineering.

WHAT IS SOCIAL ENGINEERING?

The human element, being the weakest factor in the cyber security chain, is highly susceptible to deception; hence malicious attackers adopt compromising individuals, operators and managers of information systems to grant them easy access to unauthorized data, easy compromise. Social engineering is a method of deception adopted by malicious individuals to compromise information systems by taking advantage of human weaknesses like gullibility, greed, willingness to help, curiosity, desire and fear.

Compromising victims can be in the form of manipulating unsuspecting individuals to give them unauthorized information or data like usernames, passwords or grant them logical access; or getting the victims to install malware that can compromise an information system. The manipulation comes in various forms like deceiving victims into thinking they are interacting with authorized personnel, taking advantage of victims' curiosity and desire, greed or willingness to help. The compromise can be in the form of gaining unauthorized access to certain data that can be used to achieve further goals (like obtaining access to banking information to steal funds) or could be to destroy the compromised information system or cause disruption.

QUIZ 1

1. Which of the following best explains the increased spread of cyber crime in recent times?
   a. Increased funds in the hands of criminals.
   b. Increased use and dependence on electronic media and devices.
   c. Decreased funds in the hands of criminals.

2. What is cyber security?
   a. Securing electronic devices and platforms from potential and existing threats.
   b. Methodology adopted by the Cyber men to ward off Doctor Who and his allies.
   c. Ensuring malicious individuals have easy access to electronic devices and platforms.

3. Cyber security is restricted to securing only hardware and software, devices and platforms. True or false?
   a. True.
   b. False.

4. You are as strong as your weakest link. Which of the following is the weakest link in the cyber security chain?
   a. The human element.
   b. The physical environment.
   c. Antivirus software.

5. What is social engineering?

a. The act of securing electronic devices and media to protect against potential and existing risk and threats.
b. The adoption of very advanced tools and techniques to perpetrate cyber crime targeting victims who are secured with defenses that are difficult to penetrate.
c. A method of deception adopted by malicious actors to compromise information systems by taking advantage of human weaknesses.

REFERENCES:

Rouse, M. (2016) *What is cybersecurity?* [Online]. Available from: http://whatis.techtarget.com/definition/cybersecurity (Accessed: 1 August, 2017).

WHY SOCIAL ENGINEERING?

OVERVIEW

Some major attacks occurred in 2017 which included Wannacry, Petya/NotPetya, the *Equifax* breach, and it was revealed that all *Yahoo* accounts were comprised in a previous breach. Wannacry and Petya/NotPetya were ransomware, with Wannacry affecting computer systems in over a hundred countries; and Petya/NotPetya resulted in a cost of $300 million to international shipping company *Maersk*. In 2018 among others was the leakage of over three hundred thousand transactions from *British Airways*, exposing sensitive confidential data of their customers. The term "fake news" became popular when Donald Trump became President of the United States of America. There has been a rise in cyber attacks whether targeting individuals, businesses or nation states. However, there is something that most of these attacks seem to have in common: they are mainly initiated and spread by taking advantage of human weaknesses; which makes these attacks easier and cheaper to propagate.

WHAT ARE THE MOTIVES OF SOCIAL ENGINEERS?

Social engineering is used by malicious individuals for various reasons which include:

- Making a statement
- Gaining unauthorized access to confidential information/data
- Extortion/blackmail
- Initiating attacks

The statement could be just a prank or could have political or other connotations. Some social engineers carry out social engineering solely as practical jokes to make fun of their targets, whether individuals, organizations or even nation states. These types of attacks are likely to have low-risk impact on their targets, but may also be a way of expressing ideological or political views to the target, and can affect the target in terms of reputational damage which could have adverse effects on the target's business – customers or those that patronize the target victim might end up shunning the victim; resulting in adverse effects on the victim's return on investment. Activist like environmentalists, eco-activists and others may use social engineering to gain unauthorized access to individuals or organizations they are opposed to. They can use this access to deface the victim's website, expose activities carried out by the victim which may be illegal or unethical and so on.

Malicious attackers usually use social engineering to gain access to information and data that they are not supposed to have access to, which they can further use to gain access to unauthorized data/information of victims (like online banking credentials, card details and so on). This unauthorized access can be used to steal identity, funds, confidential information (like trade secrets) and the like. Such activity could be carried out by cyber criminals to steal or organizations/nation states as part of cyber espionage, or as stated previously by activists to expose activities of their targeted victim.

Malicious attackers once they have compromised a target using social engineering can have unbridled access to confidential information and data, and can take over control of such. As a result, they can hold such data/information hostage in exchange for funds or threaten to reveal secrets contained in the data to the public if certain demands are not met; the secrets could range from trade secrets to embarrassing personal habits. Ransomware can be installed on systems by using social engineering techniques. Social engineers can leverage the data they compromise to force victims to give them what they want, like funds or assets or whatever. Leveraging compromised data can be used by criminals and activist to achieve their goals, even terrorist can adopt this. Cyber criminals would normally use this for blackmail and extortion to get funds or wealth; terrorists can use it to demand release of their comrades or get funds or arms; activists can take advantage of this to make an organization behave in a way they consider acceptable or just to punish them for not being acceptable.

A malicious attacker can not only gain access to unauthorized data via social engineering, gaining access to confidential logical access or system controls is possible; these can be used to launch attacks on a system or network using things like malware. This could be seen in the case of Stuxnet which was a malware (worm) that targeted suspected uranium enrichment systems in Iran; it was initiated using a social engineering technique. This can be considered a form of cyber warfare.

WHY IS SOCIAL ENGINEERING ADOPTED?

The easiest way to break a system is to target its weakest point- and that is the human factor. Malicious attackers adopt social engineering as a means of attaining their malicious goals because it is:

- Cheaper.
- Less complicated.
- Readily available.
- Safer.

Instead of employing very expensive IT infrastructure to carry out a malicious attack or breach on an IT system, compromising the operators of the system would be a wiser choice – it is far less expensive. Compromising the human element saves the cost and trouble of cracking codes, decryption, having to make a physical break in or physically capturing an important relevant systems operator. Going back to the case of Stuxnet on the Iranian nuclear systems, getting the systems infected by means of social engineering was cheaper than trying to get someone in to infect the systems with malware, trying to hack into the network to get it infected or trying to physically destroy the infrastructure. The cost-effectiveness of social engineering can also be seen in email scams where the scammers could be from very poor backgrounds and yet could hit a "jackpot" with little or no financial investment.

Social engineering attacks do not require a lot of sophistication to be carried out. The requirement of complicated tools and techniques for initiating attacks can be significantly reduced or even eliminated with the adoption of social engineering techniques. Social engineering is also more readily available and easier to deploy than more sophisticated attack techniques like direct hacking which could be stalled due to cost, availability of tools or the target having very good physical and electronic defenses (like firewalls, anti-malware software or anti-hacking devices).

Crimes like armed robbery or kidnapping can be very risky to life and limb of criminals; moreover they might end up not getting desired returns despite the risks taken. So for example, scammers would be more at ease engaging in the crime of scamming, patiently waiting till they strike gold; there is less stress and even if caught, the sentence is not likely to be as bad as it would be for engaging in more dangerous crimes like armed robbery, kidnapping or human trafficking. And if we refer back to the Stuxnet case again, we can see that it was easier to use social engineering to get the Iranian systems infected, sending agents in to do the job could have exposed the agents to capture or death. The agents if captured could have been broken down to reveal information which could have made the operation counterproductive. Using a mole would have also been risky, if not discovered by the Iranians, it might not be easy to discern where the mole's loyalty really lies.

THE STUXNET CASE EMPHASIZES ADOPTION OF SOCIAL ENGINEERING

The following is a brief synopsis of what occurred in the Stuxnet case:

Stuxnet, thought to have been developed in a joint operation between the United States and Israel, was a network worm that targeted suspected Iranian uranium enrichment facilities (specifically in Natanz) in 2010. It was a new type of malware in that it caused destruction of physical infrastructure as opposed to the traditional applications of such malware – only affecting information systems (Marks, 2014). The Iranian uranium enrichment infrastructure were kept off the Internet for security reasons, fear of being hacked, but this worm managed to get to the computer systems running in the uranium enrichment facility; how was that? Through USB thumb drives.

Being that the facility was off the Net, the originators of Stuxnet infected the computer systems of some companies that were contractors to the facility in Natanz probably through the Internet (Zetter, 2014). Employees in these companies used their USB drives on their systems getting them infected, and then further infected the Natanz systems when they used their drives there; the worm then proliferated over the local network in the facility. The result was the uranium enrichment centrifuges failing on an unprecedented scale (Zetter, 2014).

From the above, we see that initiators of Stuxnet saw the challenges of getting the facility in Natanz infected: it would have been very difficult to get someone there physically; it could not have been infiltrated remotely as it was not connected to the Internet; a physical assault on the facility would probably have been too costly both in terms of finance and lives. So they decided to make employees of the contractor companies unwitting couriers of the malware. We will discuss a social engineering technique called *baiting* of which there is a version that involves leaving enticing malware infected external storage media about in order to get an unsuspecting curious victim to use it on their system thereby getting them infected; this version was what was initially suspected to have been adopted to initiate the Stuxnet attack. However, the "baiting" that was applied in this case was to get unsuspecting couriers infected to get the job done.

The case of Stuxnet was initiation of attack by taking advantage of the human weaknesses inherent in the unwitting couriers of the malware. This saved the perpetrators the hassle and cost of getting access to the systems in Natanz physically or remotely; granting the malware infection easy access. It also saved them from the risk of losing agents going to the facility to carry out the act, which could have lead to capture, death or even betrayal; the cost of carrying out a physical assault was also avoided which could have also resulted in death or capture or compromise of those who would have carried out the attack or potential collateral damage.

QUIZ 2

1. What seems to have been most commonly exploited in recent cyber security attacks and breaches?
   a. Financial advancements.
   b. Human weaknesses.
   c. Software shortages.

2. Which of the following is a goal of social engineering?
   a. Crime prevention.
   b. Improve cyber security.
   c. Extortion or blackmail.

3. Malicious attackers usually use social engineering to gain access to information and data that:
   a. They are not meant to have access to.
   b. They are meant to have access to.
   c. They can definitely not use to gain further access to unauthorized information.

4. Which of the following is a reason for adopting social engineering techniques?
   a. More safe.
   b. More complicated.
   c. Less cheap.

5. How did the Iranian uranium enrichment facility in Natanz get infected with Stuxnet?
   a. Directly through the Internet.
   b. Through USB thumb drives.
   c. Via an agent that physically went there.

REFERENCES:

Marks, P. (2010) *Why the Stuxnet worm is like nothing seen before* [Online]. Available from: https://www.newscientist.com/article/dn19504-why-the-stuxnet-worm-is-like-nothing-seen-before/ (Accessed: 16 October, 2017).

Zetter, K. (2014) *An Unprecedented look at Stuxnet, the World's first Digital Weapon* [Online]. Available from: https://www.wired.com/2014/11/countdown-to-zero-day-stuxnet/ (Accessed: 16 October, 2017).

BRIEF HISTORICAL OVERVIEW

Social engineering as a matter of speaking is essentially manipulation of individual(s) to do something they would probably not have done otherwise; hence can be said to be part of human nature. There are situations where kids put on best behavior or do chores without grumbling, just to help ensure that a request they want to make will get a positive response. They may even put up a sad face when turned down hoping that will soften the adult they are requesting from; even babies cry to get attention or be fed or something. And of course even grown-ups engage in similar conduct hoping to get certain goals achieved. What has been mentioned can be seen as innocent behavior, however, there are other forms of such social engineering that are more negative in nature and could be used with criminal intent; like outright lying, deceit, sycophancy and so on. In this book social engineering is viewed strictly from the point of view of cyber security. In this chapter some old social engineering techniques which existed in the non-IT related world that the modern ones evolved from are briefly touched.

Con men, money-doublers, Ponzi schemes, impostors/impersonators, all sorts of dupes have been in existence long before the information age. Some of these malicious acts have been modified in line with current technology by malicious individuals and entities; money-doubling now comes in the form of wonderful investment schemes with over-fantastic returns promoted through email, text messages, audio/video calls, and social media; email scams are more or less a con; and so on. Human traffickers enticed people with things like job opportunities, relationships and the like as a form of bait; baiting is now a modern day social engineering technique. Even highway robbers use bait, for example having unsuspecting victims think there is someone whose car has broken down, requiring assistance, so if the unsuspecting victim stops to help, the victim gets robbed. There are some notable schemes from antiquity which can be seen to be precedent to modern day social engineering techniques. Some of these are as follow which will be discussed in this chapter:

- The Trojan horse.
- The Spanish prisoner.
- Letter from Jerusalem.
- Chain letters.
- Propaganda dissemination.

THE TROJAN HORSE

From ancient Greece came the Trojan horse. It occurred when the Greeks were at war with Troy, and pretended to abandon the war leaving a giant wooden horse behind. According to Encyclopedia Britannica (2015) when the Trojans (people of Troy) approached the horse, there was a Greek soldier there - apparently abandoned by his comrades - who informed the Trojans that the horse was meant to be an offering to the goddess of war (Athena), so the Trojans decided to take it into their city walls and celebrated their apparent victory over the Greeks. But unknown to them, the giant wooden horse was filled with Greek soldiers who eliminated the guards when the Trojans had gone to sleep, and then opened the gates signaling the rest of the Greek army to enter Troy and finish off the Trojans.

This is a precursor to modern day phishing and baiting attacks, as far as social engineering is concerned; it is also the predecessor of a malware of the same name – Trojan horse or just Trojan. The attack made use of a form of bait to lure the unsuspecting victims into thinking it was something of no harm and even of benefit, taking advantage of their gullibility and sense of victory to trick them into dropping their guard and giving the attackers unfettered access. Similarly, social engineers in cyber security terms also use techniques like baiting and phishing to trick unsuspecting victims into getting compromised.

THE SPANISH PRISONER

The Spanish prisoner, an advance fee scam which could be traced back to the late 1500's (Munson, 2016), involved scammers informing victims that there was a wealthy person who was held a prisoner in Spain, but required some financial assistance (probably to bribe corrupt guards or government officials) to help him get out. Once out, a great reward would be in store for the helper, and sometimes even his beautiful daughter would be given in marriage additionally. Pointless to say, when the victim decided to help out by offering funds, the scammer made away with the money or continued to milk the victim by implying some issues came up requiring additional funds, until the victim realizes he was being conned or the scammer becomes tired of the victim.

Fuchs (2014) pointed out one interesting thing about the Spanish Prisoner scam in an 1898 article of the New York Times (from archives) that the letters supposedly from the prisoner were written in English with a few words misspelled, and a need of an honest man to take care of his helpless daughter. We can see similar traits to these in modern day email scams, the English tends to be not so good with misspellings that indicate the author is probably not a native English speaker; there is also the tendency for the email to state that it was from a damsel in distress who needed a reliable person to help her access and secure funds from here wealthy father or something. Another thing was that the Spanish prisoner crime implied the prisoner was in a country where there was civil unrest or corruption and the like, giving impression that there were free funds available for the taking, eliciting greed in the victim.

So this scam, as its descendant the scam email, took advantage of human weaknesses of pity and willingness to help (to help out someone captured by tyrants and help his daughter), and greed/desire (desire to get rich quick with reward money and get a beautiful wife).

LETTER FROM JERUSALEM

The letter from Jerusalem is another example of an ancient advance fee fraud, this time from nineteenth century France. It involved a criminal in prison writing to aristocrats claiming to be the valet of a wealthy individual who either lost or hid some wealth (Conheady, 2014) and needed funds to help retrieve it in exchange for a handsome reward. The scammer in order to conceal identity claimed that he and his master either had hidden or abandoned a box of wealth when they were on the run, but the valet (author of the letter) was arrested when he returned to get the wealth for not having a passport, so he needed someone to help him recover the wealth and get him out of prison in exchange for a reward, claiming to have heard about the potential victim's honesty and integrity from a relative (Cima, 2015). As can be expected, the same cycle of milking the victim as in the Spanish prisoner ensues. Cima (2015) quoted Eugene Vidocq stating that the Letter from Jerusalem scam had a 20% success rate; that is 2 out of 10 people that received the letter were likely to fall victim.

This scam is also a precursor to modern day email scams, but in addition, it targeted aristocrats. This scam targeted a specific set of people, similar to spear phishing attacks that target specific types of people as well; hence it can also be seen as a precursor to spear phishing.

CHAIN LETTERS

I remember sometime in the mid-90's I got a letter, apparently photocopied, supposedly from a "Sheikh Ahmad, watchman of the prophet's tomb" containing some moral instructions. The striking thing about the letter was that at the end it stated copies should be made and circulated; that a certain person made copies and had success and progress all round, another threw it away and ended in misfortune, another forgot it in his drawer and lost his job, but upon remembering, he circulated the letter and got a far better job. I promptly torched the letter. In the early 2000's I was surprised to get the same message in email, I did some research and discovered that letter had been documented in some early Egyptian records from the early 1900's.

Chain letters usually tended to have a religious or moral connotation, and some even had financial connotations like pyramid schemes. There were those that were for a good cause, some for duping people out of money, and some came with threats of something terrible happening to anyone who received but did not spread to others, and good luck for those who did. Collins (2010) observed that one of the earliest recorded chain letters was from a Methodist women's missionary academy that were overwhelmingly in debt; the idea was for everyone receiving the letter to donate a dime to the academy, and then send the letter to at least three other people to also give similar donation and each spread to three others, having a snowball effect. The chain letter proved to be successful to the academy. Subsequently, similar methods were used for worthy causes, but with side effects like overwhelming the postal service with excess work, some people received the letter multiple times and the originators also received multiple responses from some recipients; then the con men came into the picture and used it for extorting money.

Modern day chain messages come in emails, SMS or social media messages. They may be used for email harvesting, spreading phishing messages, creating vulnerabilities on potential victims systems, extorting money through pseudo causes and so on.

PROPAGANDA DISSEMINATION

Propaganda has been used by governments and organizations from time immemorial to influence social behavior. It was used by the Nazis in Germany to influence the German public to vote them in and also instigate them against the Jewish citizens, and subsequently resulted in the Second World War. *The Last Hunter* was a movie that was centered on a propaganda method used by the Viet Cong against American soldiers during the Vietnam War; the Viet Cong broadcast a lady speaking English urging American soldiers to abandon the war and return home in order to demoralize the soldiers.

Propaganda is used to influence behavior of large number of people. One modern day application of propaganda is fake news which has been used in recent times by those in power in countries as well as those opposed to them to discredit each other.

MODERN DAY SOCIAL ENGINEERING TECHNIQUES

There are a various social engineering techniques adopted by malicious actors, a few common ones are discussed in this book namely:

- Pretexting.
- Piggy-backing.
- Shoulder surfing.
- Dumpster diving.
- Phishing.
- Scam messages.
- Baiting.
- Chain messages.
- Fake news.

Each of these will be discussed in the following chapters.

QUIZ 3

1. Which of the following is true?
   a. Social engineering is essentially waiting for someone to do what you want without any form of manipulation.
   b. Social engineering is essentially manipulation to make someone do something the person would probably not have done otherwise.
   c. Social engineering only has positive applications.

2. Which of the following is not a social engineering technique of old?
   a. Berlin wall
   b. Chain letters.
   c. Propaganda dissemination.

3. The Trojan horse can be seen as a precursor to which of the following?
   a. Antivirus software.
   b. Phishing and baiting.
   c. Scam messages.

4. The Spanish prisoner scam took advantage of which of the following human weaknesses?
   a. Intelligence, power, ability to detect fraud.
   b. Greed, desire, willingness to help.
   c. Lack of empathy for the distressed.

5. The Letter from Jerusalem and the Spanish prisoner are predecessors of which modern social engineering technique?
   a. Email scams.
   b. Piggy-backing.
   c. Dumpster diving.

6. Targeting of aristocrats associated with the Letter from Jerusalem can be seen as a precursor for:
   a. Spear phishing.
   b. Shoulder surfing.
   c. Network worms.

7. Chain letters could be used for the following except:
   a. Spread moral/religious messages.
   b. Donate funds to recipients.
   c. Extort money from recipients.

8. Propaganda dissemination as used by the Nazis in the build up to World War two can be likened to what today?
   a. Spear phishing.
   b. Pretexting.
   c. Fake news.

REFERENCES:

Cima, R. (2015) *The Email Scam with Centuries of History* [Online]. Available from:

https://priceonomics.com/the-email-scam-with-centuries-of-history/ (Accessed: 20 October, 2017).

Collins, P. (2010) *You Must Forward This Story to Five Friends: The curious history of chain letters.* [Online]. Available from: http://www.slate.com/articles/arts/culturebox/2010/10/you_must_forward _this_story_to_five_friends.html (Accessed: 22 October, 2017).

Conheady, S. (2014) Social Engineering in IT Security: Tools, Tactics, and Techniques. McGraw Hill Education.

Encyclopedia Britannica (2015) *Trojan Horse | Greek Methodology* [Online]. Available from: https://www.britannica.com/topic/Trojan-horse (Accessed: 19 October, 2017).

Fuchs, E. (2014) *Here's the 1898 Version of Those Nigerian Email Scams* [Online]. Available from:

http://www.businessinsider.com/charles-seife-writes-about-the-origin-of-the-spanish-prisoner-scam-2014-7?IR=T (Accessed: 20 October, 2017).

Munson, L. (2016) *The Spanish Prisoner: Birth of the 419 Scam* [Online]. Available from http://www.security-faqs.com/the-spanish-prisoner-birth-of-the-419-scam.html (Accessed: 20 October, 2017).

PRETEXTING

Pretexting involves a malicious attacker deceiving an unsuspecting victim by pretending to be someone else in a bid to gain unauthorized access to sensitive data and information. The social engineer may pretend to be calling from somewhere like helpdesk or IT; or pretend to be someone of higher authority. The deceit is usually carried out by calls or sometimes through messaging like email or social networks. Email spoofing can be seen as a form of pretexting, it is a kind of social engineering technique where the attacker sends an email that appears to be from a legitimate source to the victim. CEO frauds tend to be perpetrated through pretexting by way of calls or email spoofing. CEO fraud is carried out by a malicious actor deceiving victims into believing he/she is their CEO or any other senior authority then instructing them do something to achieve his/her malicious goals, for example transferring funds to an account and things like that.

The attacker would contact a victim (whether through voice calls, email or other messaging applications) claiming to be from IT helpdesk, for example, requesting for some sensitive data (like username and password, date of birth, etc) saying that the data is required for an upgrade or something similar. Once such data is acquired, it can be used to access the victim's systems and network, infiltrate to steal more sensitive data and information, siphon funds from bank accounts, install malware or add the compromised systems to a botnet. A botnet is a group of connected computer systems, media and devices under the control of a malicious individual via malware without the infected users knowing. The network can be used to carry out attacks against others for example send spam messages, click fraud campaigns, and distributed-denial-of-service attacks (Rouse, 2017).

Conheady (2014) mentioned a case in which some online brokers used pretexting to compromise Verizon Wireless. This was achieved by the brokers calling customer service and claiming to be from the special needs department of Verizon Wireless (which did not exist) and making a request on behalf of a vocally impaired customer, even using a voice distorting device to make their voice sound impaired when the Verizon Wireless customer service officer asked to speak to the customer. The result was that thousands of private mobile phone numbers of Verizon customers were released (Social Engineering, Inc., 2017). CNBC (2015) reported that money transfer company Xoom lost $30.8 million to employee impersonation (pretexting), leading to the resignation of the chief financial officer.

Pretexting takes advantage of human gullibility, willingness to assist and zeal to carry out duties. The victims easily trust others so tend to fall for scammers who pretend to be their superiors or help desk or something of that nature; they respond to such scammers because the scammers deceive them into thinking they are communicating with a genuine source, so respond to such requests with ease.

Extra vigilance and awareness of pretexting can help avoid falling victim to the technique. Employees should be educated to be wary of such techniques and to be careful of what kind of information and data they reveal to unconfirmed parties. Customers of organizations should also be enlightened as per pretexting and similar techniques, and should be made to understand what type of information and data they should not disclose unnecessarily. The customers should be educated about the kind of data that an organization will not request from them, of which if they see such requests should not oblige. Authentic numbers and lines of communication should be clearly stated to protect against both employees and customers falling victim to communication that is not from such sources.

QUIZ 4

1. Which of the following is pretexting?
   a. Peeping over someone's shoulder to illegally obtain sensitive data without the person's consent.

b. Gaining unauthorized access by informing victims of malicious intent and then initiating malicious attacks.
c. Pretending to be someone else to gain unauthorized malicious access to sensitive data and information.

2. Which of the following is an example of pretexting?
   a. CEO fraud emails.
   b. Prank calls.
   c. Botnets.

3. Pretexting's success is attributable to taking advantage of:
   a. Due diligence on the part of the victim.
   b. The victim's zeal to perform duties.
   c. The victim's lack of using malware detection tools.

4. Which of the following is not likely to help protect against pretexting?
   a. Educating employees about social engineering techniques.
   b. Educating customers about social engineering techniques.
   c. Educating both customers and employees on malware detection.

5. Enlightening both customers and employees by clearly stating lines of communication used by an organization and also letting them know what type of information or data the organization will not request from them; this can help protect against pretexting. True or false?
   a. True.
   b. False.

REFERENCES:

CNBC (2015) *Xoom says $30.8 mln transferred fraudulently to overseas accounts* [Online]. Available from: https://www.cnbc.com/2015/01/06/xoom-says-308-mln-transferred-fraudulently-to-overseas-accounts.html (Accessed: 23 October, 2017).

Conheady, S. (2014) Social Engineering in IT Security: Tools, Tactics, and Techniques. McGraw Hill Education.

Rouse, M. (2017) *botnet* [Online]. Available from: http://searchsecurity.techtarget.com/definition/botnet (Accessed: 23 October, 2017).

Social Engineering, Inc. (2017) *Vishing* [Online]. Available from: https://www.social-engineer.org/framework/attack-vectors/vishing/ (Accessed: 23 October, 2017).

PIGGY-BACKING

Piggy-backing can also be referred to as tailgating. Piggy-backing is the act of an attacker gaining unauthorized access to a restricted area by shadowing an authorized personnel, giving the impression that they are together. For example, an intruder could go to a building which has access restricted to only authorized people and tail one of them, making security personnel who control entry think he/she is with such a person, hence allowing the intruder to have a hassle-free entry and access. The attacker can also pretend to be an authorized personnel, like an employee, making it appear that he/she has forgotten his/her access card or the card is malfunctioning leading to an authorized personnel offering assistance and letting him/her into the restricted area. Chapman (2009) quoted another strain from Colin Greenless which involves the intruder just holding two cups of coffee and waiting for someone to help him/her open the door. That is to say an attacker can give the impression his/her hands are full, leading someone to render help with entry. Once a malicious attacker gains access through piggy-backing, he can steal data, install malware, or even drop a bait to entice an unsuspecting victim to install malware.

Piggy-backing takes advantage of human gullibility to deceive personnel into giving access. It also takes advantage of people's willingness to help a distressed person. There is also an element of fear, a fear of offending or embarrassing someone – security personnel may be afraid of offending/embarrassing an employee who is probably higher in rank than they are; an authorized personnel may feel not helping someone who is apparently another personnel in distress may be offending or embarrassing the person, might even feel awkward asking questions thinking "why, this can happen to me as well".

Piggy-backing can be tackled by use of methods to authorize access like identity badges, access cards, PIN codes, biometrics, dead man doors, and so on. But most importantly, security operatives and employees should be trained and enlightened about techniques used by malicious attackers like piggy-backing. The security personnel and employees should be made to understand and appreciate why they should not shy away from following laid down procedures for allowing physical access, and should ask questions, make enquiries before authorizing access in situations that are out of the ordinary – like an employee who has lost access card or has a malfunctioning card for example, even if the apparent employee is known to be a member of staff of the organization, there is the possibility that he may have been disengaged and may be trying to gain access to the organization to carry out an act of revenge or some criminal act.

QUIZ 5

1. How does piggy-backing work?
   a. An intruder shadows an authorized person as though they were together to gain unauthorized access.
   b. An intruder gains access to a restricted area by obtaining verbal or written authorization from an organization.
   c. An intruder forces his/her way past security personnel by beating them up to gain unauthorized access.

2. Which of the following is not an example of piggy-backing?
   a. An intruder pretending to be an authorized person who has lost his/her access card or the card is malfunctioning, eliciting support from an authorized person.
   b. An intruder appearing with hands full giving the impression that he/she can't reach access card, eliciting support from an authorized person.
   c. An intruder appearing to be fully armed giving the impression harm will be caused if not helped, eliciting support from an authorized person.

3. Piggy-backing takes advantage of the following human weaknesses except:
   a. Gullibility and willingness to help.
   b. Greediness and lust for power.
   c. Fear of offending or embarrassing someone.

4. Which of the following can be best be used to minimize piggy-backing?
   a. Dead man doors.
   b. Bolts on doors.
   c. Guns for guards.

5. Which of the following best helps to prevent piggy-backing?
   a. Identity badges and access cards for employees.
   b. Awareness training for security and employees.
   c. Use of biometrics and dead man doors.

REFERENCES:

Chapman, S. (2009) *Consultant Uses Social Skills to trick Corporate Security* [Online]. Available from: https://www.cio.com/article/2428266/infrastructure/consultant-uses-social-skills-to-trick-corporate-security.html (Accessed: 27 October, 2017).

SHOULDER SURFING

Shoulder surfing is the act of a malicious attacker stealing confidential and sensitive data from unsuspecting victims essentially by looking over the victims shoulder. The main thing about shoulder surfing is that the attacker steals the data without the victim being aware, this can be achieved by simply peeping over the victim's shoulder, using hidden cameras, installing keystroke loggers, ATM skimmers, and the like. An intruder could steal usernames, passwords or PIN codes which they can use to compromise their victims and take over their access, or steal data or funds. So shoulder surfing can be defined as a method of stealing confidential and sensitive data (like login credentials) by using a form of surveillance or the other (the surveillance could be peeping over shoulder, using hidden camera or skimmers and so on).

Criminals have been known to install hidden cameras at ATM points to steal card PINs as they are being entered. They also install fake keypads on ATMs used to collect card details, ATM skimmers can be inserted in card slots to steal card data, and cash traps can also be installed at ATM cash dispense units. Krebs on security (2013) gave an example of a skimmer found November 2013 in Brazil which was a complete fake ATM placed over the real one at a bank. The customers would insert their cards and enter PINs only to get apparent error messages, not knowing that their card details and PINs have been compromised. Cash traps are installed in an ATM's cash dispense area, the traps resemble the shutter that is normally there; hence do not arouse suspicion, they block any cash that is dispensed from the machine giving the withdrawing customer the impression there is some kind of dispense error or malfunction. Once the customer is gone and the area is free of witnesses, the criminal removes the cash trap with the dispensed cash stuck in it. Cash traps are not a shoulder surfing technique, by the way.

Shoulder surfing takes advantage of victims' sense of security, inattentiveness and negligence. The victims usually feel they are in their comfort zones so expect that nothing is likely to go wrong; hence their guard is down, giving the attacker an upper hand.

The menace of shoulder surfing can be tackled with alertness and extra vigilance. In office environments where there are cubicles that are not see-through, employees should avoid leaving their doors open (especially when entering login credentials on their computing endpoints). Institutions that maintain ATMs (like banks) should educate both their employees and customers on entering PINs discretely (covering the keypad with the other hand when entering the PIN is a good idea) such that someone behind cannot peep to see what is being typed. The organizations should also further educate both employees and customers on detecting surveillance devices like hidden cameras and also how to detect skimmers. When going to withdraw cash from an ATM, it would be wise to wiggle everything from the keypad to the card insertion point to ensure that they is not something stuck on the actual points in order to steal data, like skimmers. Criminals tend to install cash traps, skimmers and cameras during times when banks are closed for long periods and there is high ATM traffic, like weekends and holidays, and then take them off at the end of such periods (Krebs on security, 2013). Those periods not only have more likely victims using the machines, but also it is less likely that there will be personnel attending to the machines during the periods, decreasing the chances of detection. Therefore, there is the need for further and extra vigilance during such periods. Banks should ensure there are adequate personnel deployed to such sensitive areas during such period, and use of CCTV cameras can help deter the criminal actions.

QUIZ 6

1. Which of the following best describes shoulder surfing?
   a. Malicious attackers stealing confidential and sensitive data from unsuspecting victims by pretending to be authorized personnel.

b. Malicious attackers stealing confidential and sensitive data from unsuspecting victims by using a form of surveillance.
c. Malicious attackers stealing confidential and sensitive data from unsuspecting victims by shadowing authorized personnel.

2. Which of the following is an example of shoulder surfing?
   a. Attacker using software to guess usernames and passwords.
   b. Attacker placing a false keypad on ATM to steal card data.
   c. Attacker claiming to be customer service to steal logon credentials.

3. Shoulder surfing takes advantage of:
   a. Fear and insecurity.
   b. Negligence and inattentiveness.
   c. Willingness to help and gullibility.

4. Which of the following can ensure shoulder surfing is successful?
   a. Alertness and extra vigilance.
   b. Covering keypad when typing.]
   c. Exposing keypad when typing.

5. Why should there be extra vigilance when using ATMs during weekends or holidays?
   a. Machines are likely to have less attention by maintainers then, and there is likely to be higher customer traffic.
   b. Machines are likely to have more attention by the maintainers and there is likely to be higher customer traffic.
   c. Machines are likely to have covers to block peeping and there would be devices installed to detect cameras and skimmers.

REFERENCES:

Krebs on Security (2013) *The Biggest Skimmers of All: Fake ATMs* [Online]. Available from: https://krebsonsecurity.com/2013/12/the-biggest-skimmers-of-all-fake-atms/ (Accessed: 29 October, 2017).

DUMPSTER DIVING

Dumpster diving involves malicious attackers checking through garbage for sensitive data or information that was not properly discarded. Sensitive data can also easily fall into the hands of malicious attackers if they are left laying around carelessly, like invoices, receipts and storage media containing confidential data left carelessly about the place, employee data left in the same way, passwords on sticky note stuck on systems and devices that require such passwords to operate, and things like that.

Steve Hunt, a security industry analyst, decided to go through the garbage of a major bank and within three minutes, he was able to find sensitive documents, and even a laptop (Goodchild, 2009). The documents included a copy of a cheque, documents showing financial transactions, and sensitive personally identifiable information of customers which in the hands of a malicious individual can constitute a major tragedy.

Dumpster diving takes advantage of victims' misplaced sense of security and negligence. There is usually a feeling that nobody will go through what has been discarded; hence effort is usually not made to completely obliterate what is contained in disposed material.

To guard against dumpster diving, effort has to be made to ensure that documents, devices, instruments and anything containing data that is to be discarded are properly disposed off such that any sensitive data contained therein is irretrievable. Employees should be compelled to properly dispose any sensitive material or items that contain anything sensitive, and they should be made to understand and appreciate why. They should also be made to understand that documents and systems should not be left about carelessly which increases the risk of them getting compromised. Paper documents should be discarded by shredding both vertically and horizontally or completely burning to ashes as opposed to just dropping in bin, crumpling, or shredding in only one direction. Electronic media should be thoroughly destroyed physically such that recovery becomes impossible. Disks may be wiped and then formatted several times over to avoid possibility of data recovery from such disks or they may be demagnetized. Demagnetization is a method of completely destroying what is contained on a hard disk by using magnetic fields.

QUIZ 7

1. Which of the following involves searching through garbage for sensitive data and information?
   a. Piggy-backing.
   b. Shoulder surfing.
   c. Dumpster diving.

2. Documents and storage media containing sensitive information should be kept where they can be easily accessed by anyone, and passwords can be written on devices where they are input to aid remembrance. True or false?
   a. True.
   b. False.

3. Dumpster diving takes advantage of victims' misplaced sense of security and negligence. True or false?
   a. True.
   b. False.

4. Which of the following would benefit a dumpster diver?
   a. Burning discarded paper documents to ashes.

b. Shredding discarded paper documents both vertically and horizontally.
c. Crumpling discarded paper documents.

5. Which of the following will best protect a discarded hard disk from dumpster diving?
a. Demagnetization.
b. Formatting once.
c. Deletion of all files.

REFERENCES:

Goodchild, J. (2013) *A Real Dumpster Dive: Banks Tosses Personal Data, Checks, Laptops* [Online]. Available from: https://www.csoonline.com/article/2123810/identity-theft-prevention/a-real-dumpster-dive--bank-tosses-personal-data--checks--laptops.html (Accessed: 29 October, 2017).

PHISHING

Phishing is a deceptive technique that uses communication channels to imitate a known genuine source in order to gain unauthorized access by directing to a point that will compromise a victim. It is quite similar to pretexting as both make an appearance of being from a genuine source, but the most common way of propagating it is through messaging systems like email. Phishing is usually used to steal sensitive data like login credentials, online banking details or payment card details. Phishing messages usually come with a link or an attachment. The link could be made to appear like it is from a genuine source, like your bank, and clicking may result in a webpage that is an exact replica of the website it claims to be (like your bank's online banking logon page); the page would include the space for username and password, which if you enter ensures you are compromised. The link may open or open to an error page or not even open at all making it appear as though there was an error, but the result of the clicking is installation of malware on the system; attachments also have a similar result. The malware can be used for various attacks, like stealing login credentials, taking over logical access, adding the compromised system and/or network to a botnet and so on.

Phishing can come in various forms other than through email messages like SMS messages or social media messages and so on. Phishing carried out through SMS is known as **smishing** and can get an individual or the individual's mobile device compromised or lead to a fraudulent site to steal data. Another form of phishing is **vishing**, which is carried out using voice messages that can direct to fraudulent URLs or get systems infected. Phishing is usually directed towards random targets, but those targeted towards a specific set of people, like high net worth customers of a specific bank, is known as **spear phishing** – we had mentioned in the brief historical overview chapter that the letter from Jerusalem could be seen as a precursor to spear phishing.

Phishing takes advantage of human gullibility and lack of awareness. Some phishing messages may state that someone's account would be blocked if necessary action is not taken by clicking a link or following instructions in an attachment; these types of attacks also take advantage of fear – fear of losing something. Figure 1 shows an example of a phishing email claiming to be from a bank requesting a link be clicked to complete an upgrade:

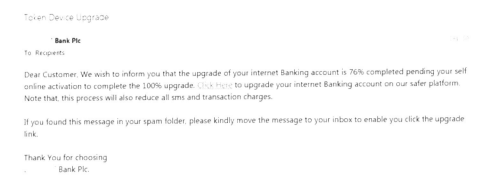

Figure 1: Sample phishing email

Figure 2: Sample smishing message.

Figure 2 shows an example of a smishing message which tries to lure victims by making them believe their mobile number won a large amount of money from Coca-Cola. It requests name, age and mobile number to be sent to a bogus email address that it supposed to be Coca-Cola's; this gives the scammers the opportunity to obtain PII in the form of requested data. If the number actually won something, there wouldn't really be any need to request for it; moreover the potential victim should contemplate whether he/she entered into any Coca-Cola promo with their mobile number in the first place. The email address provided is also a giveaway, a big corporation like Coca-Cola is obviously not going to use a free email service like *live.com*, they would rather have their own domain based email, that is to say the name of the company would be reflected in the email domain. This message tries to take advantage of greed and probably desperation on the part of the victims, offering them a get rich quick opportunity, to lure them into getting their data compromised.

To protect against phishing, avoid clicking on links or opening attachments from unknown sources; and even those apparently from known sources without some level of confirmation; hover your mouse cursor over a link to show you the actual URL. The wording of messages would likely not be that used by the person the message is supposedly from, but even if you cannot decipher the wording you can contact the apparent sender to ensure whether the person sent such message. Bottom line: phishing can best be tackled with awareness. Organizations should educate their employees and customers on phishing to help them avoid falling victim. Organizations in the financial sector, like banks, usually send messages to their customers to avoid clicking links sent to them for banking transactions, but rather to go straight to the bank's website and initiate any transaction from there; they also notify their customers that they would not send messages requesting sensitive data to them.

QUIZ 8

1. Which of the following is similar to pretexting in terms of appearing to be from a genuine source?
   a. Shoulder surfing.
   b. Piggy-backing.
   c. Phishing.

2. Which of the following best describes phishing?

a. A deceptive technique used to gain unauthorized access using communication channels, appearing to be from a genuine source, which lead victims to something that can compromise them like a link or attachment.
b. A deceptive technique used to gain unauthorized access to a restricted area by shadowing authorized personnel, giving the impression of being together with such person(s).
c. A deceptive technique used to gain unauthorized access using communication channels, appearing to be from a genuine source, which lead victims to believe they are communicating with authorized personnel.

3. Which of the following is not likely to be contained in a phishing message?
   a. A link to a fraudulent site that is an exact replica of a known genuine website.
   b. A link or attachment that leads to victims being infected with malware.
   c. A link leading to a genuine news website highlighting a disaster that occurred.

4. Which of the following is phishing carried out using mobile phone text messages?
   a. Vishing.
   b. Smishing.
   c. Spear phishing.

5. Which of the following are weaknesses phishing takes advantage of?

a. Fear of losing something and gullibility.
b. Fear of appearing offensive or rude.
c. Fear of getting rich quick.

6. Which of the following can make one become a victim of phishing?
   a. Avoid clicking links and downloading attachments from unknown sources, especially when not what is normally received.
   b. Avoid clicking links and downloading attachments from known sources not consistent with what the known source would send.
   c. Avoid heeding to advice not to click on links and attachments that are from unknown sources or not consistent with what is normally received.

SCAM MESSAGES

Scam messages also known as advance fee fraud messages, Nigerian letter, letter from a Nigerian prince or 419 scam messages involve scammers tricking victims into sending them money in anticipation of receiving far more money in return. The name 419 (four-one-nine) scam emanates from section 419 of chapter 38 of the Nigerian criminal code pertaining to obtaining property under false pretence and cheating (International Centre for Nigerian Law, 2017); and the term 4-1-9 is also used as a slang in Nigeria denoting fraud or scam. There is a tendency for the perpetrators of the crime to be of Nigerian origin, hence the reference to the Nigerian criminal code and also the name "Nigerian letter", but the perpetrators are not only Nigerians, and the scams do not originate from only Nigeria. There was the case of 67 year old Michael Neu of Louisiana in the USA who was arrested in 2017 for being part of a 419 scam gang (Ventura, 2017) – a break from the stereotype of Nigerians as scammers. As discussed in the brief historical overview, the Spanish prisoner scam and the letter from Jerusalem were precedents to scam messages.

The scam messages usually come in email or social media messages (which may still refer back to email) supposedly coming from a wealthy person in a country devastated by natural or human disasters (earthquake, flood, war, corruption, etc) claiming there is some wealth stuck somewhere which can only be accessed after certain payments are made. The scammer seeks victims that will make such payments which are a very small fraction of the stuck wealth in return for a reward that will more than cover the expenses involved in making that payment.

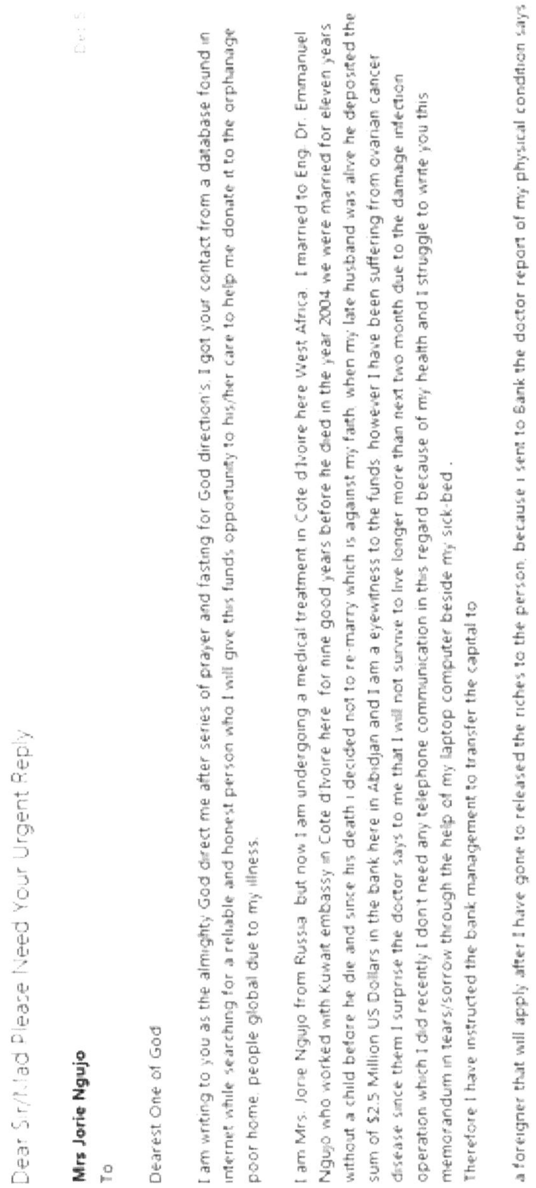

Dec 5

Dear Sir/Mad Please Need Your Urgent Reply

Mrs Jorie Ngujo
To

Dearest One of God

I am writing to you as the almighty God direct me after series of prayer and fasting for God direction's. I got your contact from a database found in internet while searching for a reliable and honest person who I will give this funds opportunity to his/her care to help me donate it to the orphanage poor home people global due to my illness.

I am Mrs. Jorie Ngujo from Russia but now I am undergoing a medical treatment in Cote d'Ivoire here West Africa. I married to Eng. Dr. Emmanuel Ngujo who worked with Kuwait embassy in Cote d'Ivoire here for nine good years before he died in the year 2004 we were married for eleven years without a child before he die and since his death I decided not to re-marry which is against my faith. when my late husband was alive he deposited the sum of $2.5 Million US Dollars in the bank here in Abidjan and I am a eyewitness to the funds however I have been suffering from ovarian cancer disease since then I surprise the doctor says to me that I will not survive to live longer more than next two month due to the damage infection operation which I did recently I don't need any telephone communication in this regard because of my health and I struggle to write you this memorandum in tears/sorrow through the help of my laptop computer beside my sick-bed .
Therefore I have instructed the bank management to transfer the capital to

a foreigner that will apply after I have gone to released the riches to the person. because i sent to Bank the doctor report of my physical condition says I will not survived longer. and I took this decision because i don't have any child that will inherit this money and my husband relatives are immoral unbeliever and I don't want my husband s hard earned money to be misused by unbelievers and also be conscious to know that the account

Figure 3: Sample scam email

A common strain of the email scams involves a message being received on social media, like Facebook, appearing to be from a lady apparently seeking a relationship. The lady states that she prefers to communicate through email and offers an email for the communication. If her message receives a positive reply, she introduces herself and even sends pictures claiming she is looking for a relationship. When another positive response is received regarding her plight, she then states that she is from a country ravaged by war (like Libya, Syria, South Sudan and so on) and the daughter of an influential wealthy leader who was killed in the war (might even include a link to a genuine news website showing that such a wealthy influential leader was killed) and that her father bequeathed his wealth to her (stating a very large sum of money, probably amassed illegally). She claims to be a refugee in somewhere like Cote D'Ivoire under the care of a Reverend and that she cannot access her inherited wealth without a trustee. Hence; she requires the victim to be the trustee in exchange for a share of the wealth, but there would be some fees that have to be paid first by the trustee before the funds can be released by the bank that holds the wealth. If the payment is made, the scammer would probably continue giving excuses for more payments to be made and continue milking the victim until the scammers decides he has had enough of the victim or the victim realizes it is con.

The scammers are commonly referred to as "Yahoo boys", and such email scams known as "Yahoo-yahoo" in Nigeria. They usually consider themselves to be modern day Robin Hoods stealing from the "greedy rich" and giving to the poor (although in reality they are more like Robin Brain from 90's cartoon show *Pinky and the Brain* who stole from the rich and gave to himself). The scammers take advantage of not only greed to defraud their victims, but pity and willingness to help as well.

In order to avoid falling victim of email scams, ignore unsolicited offers, especially offers that appear too good to be true. There is also a tendency for some scams to claim being from a person of Semitic middle-eastern or North-African origin, yet the person's picture depicts a black West-African; the English and syntax of the message are also

Guide to Social Engineering

sometimes not very good. Being aware of such details should help keep from falling victim to email scams.

QUIZ 9

1. Which of the following best describes scam messages?
   a. Messages sent trying to trick victims into sending advance payment in anticipation of more money in return.
   b. Messages sent trying to trick victims into clicking on fraudulent links or attachments that lead to monetary loss.
   c. Messages sent to victims directing to a certain website claiming they won a something like a jackpot, to end up conned.

2. Which of the following are possible signs of a 419 scam message?
   a. A lady claiming to be from IT helpdesk informing that she requires your full name, gender, date of birth, address, phone number and employee number in order to ensure your system's access is not loss due to an update.
   b. A lady claiming to be the only surviving heir of a deceased influential wealthy person from a war-torn country requiring your assistance to be a trustee for her to be able to access her inheritance, and promising a handsome reward in return.
   c. A lady claiming she had forgotten her access card in the office when she went out for lunch; hence requiring that you assist her by helping her get into your organization's building which has restricted access.

3. Scam messages take advantage of:
   a. Greed, willingness to help and pity.
   b. Apathy and fear of the unknown.
   c. Doubtfulness, anger, suspicion.

4. The following are signs of a typical scam message except:
   a. Offers that appear too good to be true.
   b. Picture showing a different race from claimed nationality.
   c. Advice not to click on suspicious links.

5. Which of the following is slang for 419 email scammers in Nigeria?
   a. Robin Hood.
   b. Yahoo boys.
   c. Robin Brain.

REFERENCES:

International Centre for Nigerian Law (2017) *Criminal Code Act-Part IV to the end* [Online]. Available from: http://www.nigeria-law.org/Criminal%20Code%20Act-Part%20VI%20%20to%20the%20end.htm (Accessed: 1 November, 2017).

Ventura, C. (2017) Police arrest alleged "Nigerian Prince" email scammer in Louisiana. *USA Today*, [online]. Available from: https://www.usatoday.com/story/news/nation-now/2017/12/30/nigerian-prince-email-scammer-louisiana/992073001/ (Accessed: 18 September, 2018).

BAITING

Baiting involves a malicious actor using a form of enticement to lure unsuspecting victims into installing malware on their endpoint and/or network. An example of baiting is clickbait that is common on video sites like Youtube where a video has a thumbnail that elicits the curiosity of individuals leading them to view the video, only to discover that the thumbnail has little or no correlation to the video. Such techniques are used on Youtube and the likes to generate traffic for the video uploader whether for the number of views or for viewers to see the video which could be an advert or promotion or something like that, or just a prank. However, the baiting can have more sinister applications like malware infections as stated.

Baiting can come in the form of messages (whether email, social media or SMS), flashing banners, pop-up messages, or carefully placed or labeled storage media. Baiting by way of messages normally comes with an enticing link or attachment which contains malware that can infect victims, compromising the victims' systems and probably organization/network or links could be used to direct victims to a fraudulent site (this means phishing messages are a form of baiting, as they use enticement in the form of links and attachments). Some websites or apps may have flashing banners or pop-up messages that attract victims' attention and curiosity, like job opportunities, a way to make quick money, pornography, malware detection and so on, which when clicked lead to compromise of endpoints and networks. The method of baiting by way of storage media usually involves the malicious attacker placing storage media like flash drives, optical disks, memory cards and so on in strategic places that could be easily noticed by an organization's employees; the bait might be labeled with enticing labels like senior management payrolls or bonuses, promotion lists, systems update, anti-virus, even pornography to get the employees to try viewing what is on these media on their endpoints, resulting in malware infection of systems and the network.

E-whoring is an example of baiting that is common. It is perpetrated by an individual claiming to be a person willing to show off sexually explicit pictures or videos to potential victims in order to lure them to something like a porn site or dating site, or to blackmail victims. Blackmail can be done by threatening to disclose to others (like family, friends or employers) that the victim was interested in indulging in something like pornography. E-whoring can be used to obtain compromising pictures or videos of the victim, this achieved by the perpetrator claiming that he/she would send desirous videos or pictures to the victim if similar of the victim are received. These media can be used to blackmail the victim.

Panda Security (2012) detected a Facebook worm that was spread by way of bait claiming to be a leaked video of a celebrity couple's home. When victims clicked the video, instead of playing it led them to a fraudulent Facebook page asking them to install a plug-in that would enable them view the video which would get the victims infected and the bait shared with all the victim's contacts (Panda Security, 2012). Another example was a Facebook clickbait worm described by Souza (2015) which came in the form of an article as bait. When the article is clicked a pop-up message comes asking to like the article's Facebook page with an "X" button on the top right corner supposedly signifying a cancel button, liking would initiate malware infection and canceling the same; that is to say anything clicked on the pop-up is a bait leading to infection. Similarly, this malware also shares the bait to all the victim's Facebook friends.

Figure 4: Sample baiting email

Baiting primarily takes advantage of human curiosity. It also takes advantage of human weaknesses like desire, lust, greed and desperation. Bait like those claiming to lead to relationships like dating sites and pornography take advantage of desire and lust; get rich quick bait takes advantage of greed; while those offering job opportunities could take advantage of desperation and helplessness. Low self-esteem may also be manipulated with quick weight loss or beauty enhancement bait.

Baiting attacks can best be avoided by awareness. Other factors that can help protect against falling victim of baiting include self-control, patience, and improved self-esteem.

QUIZ 10

1. What is baiting?
    a. A social engineering technique that entices unsuspecting victims into making advance payments in anticipation of a financial reward.
    b. A social engineering technique that uses a form of enticement to lure unsuspecting victims into installing malware on their systems.
    c. A social engineering technique that deceives unsuspecting victims into verbally revealing sensitive data by way of audio communication.

2. Baiting can be used to cause malware infection using the following except:
    a. Links in emails or pop-up windows.
    b. Strategically placed infected disks.
    c. Hidden cameras and keyloggers.

3. Which of the following can help guard against baiting?

a. Self control.
b. Low self esteem.
c. Desperation.

4. Baiting mainly takes advantage of:
    a. Self control.
    b. Awareness.
    c. Curiosity.

5. Which of the following is the best defense against baiting?
    a. Dead man door.
    b. Awareness.
    c. CCTV cameras.

REFERENCES:

Panda Security (2012) *Katy Perry and Russell Brand Used as Bait to Spread New Facebook Worm, According to Panda Labs* [Online]. Available from: https://www.pandasecurity.com/mediacenter/press-releases/katy-perry-and-russell-brand-used-as-bait-to-spread-new-facebook-worm-according-to-pandalabs/ (Accessed: 2 November, 2017).

Souza, F (2015) *Analyzing a Facebook Clickbait Worm* [Online]. Available from: https://blog.sucuri.net/2015/06/analyzing-a-facebook-clickbait-worm.html (Accessed: 2 November. 2017).

CHAIN MESSAGES

We had seen earlier that chain letters of old had evolved into modern day chain messages using communication media like email, social media and SMS to proliferate by malicious attackers in order to achieve their malicious goals. Chain messages are messages sent using various communication media which lead victims to spread the message to others; leading to an exponential increase in the spread of such messages. Sometimes these messages keep circulating for many years. Malicious individuals use chain messages to achieve varying goals: a chain message can be used to spread malware or compromise victims using phishing techniques; mislead victims into damaging their systems; spread things like malice, mistrust, fear, confusion or stir public opinion; get email addresses to use for further attacks and so on. Chain messages are usually based on some kind of sentiment, belief, superstition or just fun. They may also use some form of bait to entice victims to the message. They tend to end with an encouragement to forward to other people (some even request copying the sender when forwarding), or come in a format that the victim cannot help but forward to others, who would similarly do the same.

Some chain messages that have been circulating, usually through email and other text-based messaging media, include phishing links or attachments. The messages can be for something like virus alert. Recipients might immediately forward such messages to people they feel may find it beneficial even without clicking the links or attachments themselves, but those whom might be in need of what is sent would probably do so and send to more friends and relatives. The links/attachments may result in phony pages or documents which would be laced with malware. Virus hoaxes like the jdbgmgr.exe email hoax can ask victims to delete certain systems files by informing them that the file is a virus and they would probably be infected because they are in the sender's mail list and describe how to access the file (Christensen, 2017), the file is an actual Windows file and not a virus, so when victims see it, they are automatically convinced they are infected and delete the file. The jdbgmgr.exe was generally harmless, but a malicious attacker can send such a message referring to a crucial security file as a virus, which when deleted would make the victims susceptible to malware infections or provide the attacker easy access to their systems. Such a message is very likely to spread even if there are no instructions to forward to all contacts, as the initial message informs the victims that they are receiving such because they are part of the sender's mail list, hence the victims also automatically would forward the message to those on their mail lists as well.

Chain messages could come in the form of a message asking that it should be forwarded to others in order to get some good luck or avoid bad luck; could be a joke, health tip, religious advice asking that it should be spread to others; if the messages contain links or attachments, there is a high probability that they contain phishing malware. Some of the messages may end with "forward to others including the person who sent to you", these could be so that the malicious attacker can harvest email addresses as some may even instruct use of the "Reply All" option and copy more recipients. The attacker can use this to gain knowledge of whom and who are connected and can use that to initiate attacks targeting victims that are within a particular circle of friends. There have been messages claiming to be from *Yahoo* or similar platforms claiming that the recipient's account would be canceled if the message is not forwarded to a large number of recipients, eliciting use of "Reply All" and copy more people, giving the attacker a good database of recipient and his/her contacts.

There are chain messages that are initiated to spread some form of propaganda in the grapevine. These types don't target systems, but people. They can be used to influence public opinion, or set people against one another, could lead to civil unrest and things like that. A nation state can use this kind of chain message to direct what happens in another nation state in a certain way, like swing elections in a certain direction, spread mutual distrust setting certain demographics against others, such that things move how this manipulating nation state wants in line with their own interests.

Some weaknesses chain messages take advantage of include lack of awareness, ignorance, willingness to help, sentiments, beliefs and zealousness. The victims will likely circulate chain messages out of lack of awareness and ignorance of what the messages contain and the phenomenon of chain messages as a whole. The victims are usually zealously trying to help out their friends and acquaintance, so they forward the messages out of concern for the recipients. Sentiments in the messages and the belief they appear to promote also ginger victims to spread the messages the more.

Figure 4 shows an actual chain message that was spread in Nigeria at the close of 2017. It claims to offer a free Christmas voucher (the bait) from *Jumia* (*Jumia* is a popular online shopping site in Nigeria) to victims requiring them to click a link which leads to a site that requests the message be forwarded to many people and *WhatsApp* groups for the voucher to be redeemed. This was used to get the link spread and probably used to harvest *WhatsApp* numbers and/or infect them. The thing about the link contained in the message was the URL "*jumia.com.ng.new-vouchers.win*"; the actual URL of Jumia is "*jumia.com.ng*". For those that were unaware, the site appeared to be the actual URL of *Jumia*, but in reality the fake site had what appeared to be *Jumia's* domain as the subdomain, the main domain being "*new-voucher.win*". A subdomain appears before a main domain of a website – that is to the left – to show it is under the main domain which is at the end, to the right. This can be seen when one registers for a free website domain on sites like *Wix* and *Wordpress* where the chosen name by the registrant shows up before the *Wix* or *Wordpress* domain. Having an understanding these kinds of concepts helps to avoid falling for such tricks.

Awareness is the best medicine against chain messages. There is a need to think twice before forwarding messages to others and be sure of what the message contains, especially when the message asks to be forwarded to others, and even more so when it asks to copy the sender or use "Reply All" button. It should be borne in mind that organizations like *Yahoo* are not going to ask anyone to forward messages to all their contacts or as many people as possible in order to avoid an account being blocked or cancelled.

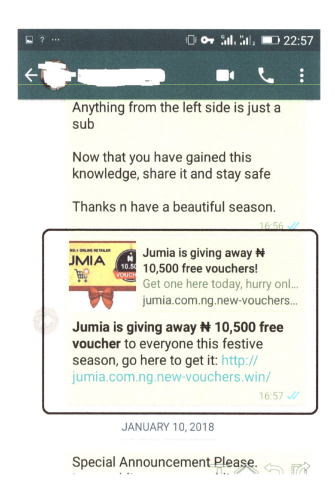

Figure 5: sample chain message from WhatsApp.

QUIZ 11

1. Which of the following best describes chain messages?
   a. Messages sent to victims encouraging them to send to more contacts making the messages spread exponentially.

b. Messages sent to victims encouraging them to send money so as to get some funds released promising a great reward in return.

c. Messages sent to victims encouraging them to click links or attachments that result in the victims being infected with malware.

2. Which of the following can malicious actors achieve using chain messages? Choose best answer.
   a. Malware infestation.
   b. Stir public opinion.
   c. Both of the above.

3. What could be the motive behind a message asking that it should be forwarded to all contacts and copy the sender?
   a. Email harvesting.
   b. None whatsoever.
   c. Password theft.

4. Chain messages do not take advantage of lack of awareness, ignorance, willingness to help, sentiments or beliefs. True or false?
   a. True.
   b. False.

5. Online communication channels like *Yahoo*, *WhatsApp* or *Gmail* may from time-to-time request you forward an email to all your contacts and as many people as possible to avoid your account being blocked. True or false?
   a. True.
   b. False.

REFERENCES:

Christensen, B.M. (2017) *Teddy Bear Virus Hoax - jdbgmgr.exe* [Online]. Available from: http://www.hoax-slayer.net/teddy-bear-virus-hoax-jdbgmgr-exe/ (Accessed: 3 November, 2017).

FAKE NEWS

Propaganda dissemination has become much easier with advancements in communication systems like email, SMS, instant messaging and social media. Fake news are false stories that are initiated to spread untrue issues in such a way that a large number of people can be influenced in a certain direction, a form of propaganda dissemination. The term fake news became staple when Donald Trump became President of the United States as he used the term to refer to the propaganda used by those considered opposed to him who had control of the media. From the President's perspective, these media moguls were using fake news to stir public opinion against him, while they on their part similarly accused the President of using fake news to set the people against them.

Fake news can be used to cause civil disorder; it can set up people against one another bringing about breakdown in law and order. Fake news can be adopted as a cyber warfare technique; there were allegations that Russia influenced the direction of elections that brought President Trump into power by spreading unfavorable information about his opponent while painting him in a good light. Some considered this alleged act by Russia as a form of cyber war. Chain messages can be used to spread fake news.

Fake news is propagated by taking advantage of human weaknesses of trust, lack of awareness, ignorance, willingness to help, sentiments, beliefs and zealousness. Victims usually trust the source of the news which leads them to be spread exponentially. The recipients would trust the sender, who trusted the source usually a website or news seen on social media. The senders keep sending believing they are doing the recipients a favor by making them aware of what they think is happening. The fake news usually takes advantage of beliefs and sentiments that are for example religious or racist in nature by being crafted along the lines of these; the recipients in their zeal then spread the news more and more. In Nigeria 2018, fake news was spread on *WhatsApp* about a health worker with her picture depicted as a child trafficker, she reported to the police and some of those who were spreading the message were arrested. She was lucky. In India an individual was lynched as a result fake news spread on *WhatsApp* depicting a picture of him similar to the health worker. This lynching led to *WhatsApp* indicating *"forwarded"* on messages that are forwarded to help ease such falsehood being considered true, and the forwarding limited to twenty recipients; and five recipients in India (Hern, 2018).

Some fake news use images and videos from an actual incident that occurred and present it as something else. There was an example of a video from India showing workers of a company protesting non-payment of their wages by picketing the company's property including solar panels it used for power generation. This video was resent by some individuals and presented as villagers who were provided with electrify via solar, but their priest informed them that the panels annoy their "Sun god", so they decided to destroy the "blasphemous" things. The phenomenon of deep fakes is another avenue that can be used to generate fake news. Deep fakes are used to edit videos kind of like *Photoshop* is used for editing images; hence the head of an individual can be superimposed in a video of someone else giving the impression that the individual was engaged in an act whereas he/she was not. Deep fake software was surprisingly easy to obtain and posed a potential risk of creating civil disturbances. There is also software that can be used to edit a video to lip-synch to a statement, which could be applied to make a person appear to say something he/she didn't.

Most fake news tend to be spread in social media messages which at best only claim to be sourced from a known trusted news outlet, without a link to the outlet; or they come from so-called alternative news sites that are not known for making efforts to authenticate news. Some may also be just what someone sees on social media like FaceBook and decides to spread; there are even those that were originally intended as a joke but the original recipient assumed it was real and spread to others. During the Ebola outbreak in 2014, a lady sent a joke in a message to a friend indicating that bathing with salt would protect from being infected by the virus; the friend forwarded the message, thinking that was a fact, and it spread like wildfire resulting in individuals bathing with salt and some lost their lives as a result.

To protect against falling victim of fake news, checking that a *WhatsApp* message is forwarded is one, but it should be borne in mind that the message can be copied and sent individually to others instead of forwarding to eliminate discarding of the message based on this check. The best way to counter fake news is to search for such news on the site of the news outlet it claims to be from, and even if there is not source stated (which is a pointer to it being fake) searching known and established conventional well-known and trusted news sites can be used to confirm, if the news is real they will most likely not miss out on reporting it based on the content contained. However, there is a need for extra vigilance regarding any news item that can be instigating even if reported by a trusted media outlet as the outlets tend to serve the interest of their owners.

QUIZ 12

1. Fake news is creation of stories to spread untrue issues such that a large number of people can get influenced by the message contained in it. True or false?
   a. True.
   b. False.

2. Fake news can be used for the following except:
   a. Cyber warfare.
   b. Influence public opinion.
   c. Verify veracity of rumors.

3. Fake news takes advantage of which of the following human weaknesses?
   a. Greed.

b. Ignorance.
c. Lust.

4. Which of the following can best help prevent falling victim of fake news?
   a. Check for the story on trusted sites and media.
   b. Check that you trust the sender.
   c. Check if the story is on social media.

5. The term "fake news" was popularized by:
   a. The Ukrainian crisis.
   b. President Donald Trump.
   c. Alleged Russian interferences.

REFERENCES:

Hern, A. (2018) WhatsApp to restrict message forwarding after India mob lynchings. *The Guardian*, [online]. Available from: https://www.theguardian.com/technology/2018/jul/20/whatsapp-to-limit-message-forwarding-after-india-mob-lynchings (Accessed: 18 September, 2018).

CONCLUSION

Malicious individuals and entities have increasingly adopted electronic devices and platforms as mediums for carrying out attacks, and targets for their malicious goals. They could also target these devices and platforms not as the end targets, but as a stepping stone to achieve their dubious objectives. Targeting these devices and platforms is by no means an easy task, and could require very expensive tools and scarce difficult to attain expertise for attackers to be able to penetrate their targets, however, this bottleneck can be side-stepped by targeting the weakest link as far as these devices and platforms are concerned – that is the human factor. Human weaknesses can be easily exploited by malicious attackers to achieve their malicious goals. Criminals and adversarial nation states have found that it is cheaper, less complicated and safer to adopt social engineering to at least initiate attacks.

Exploiting human weaknesses in order to achieve criminal or malicious objectives is definitely not a new domain; it has been around from time immemorial. It is from these previous techniques that modern day applications of social engineering evolved – the likes of the "Spanish Prisoner", "Letter from Jerusalem", chain messages and other cons. These cons of old have shown that human weaknesses can be exploited at any time and the perseverance of the modern ones shows that technology is useless in protecting against them if the protection is not in conjunction with strengthening the human factor against its weaknesses – you are as strong as your weakest link.

In order to be safe from the menace of social engineering, individuals and organizations need to be aware of how it can be used to exploit them. If you are aware of threats against you and how they manifest, that will make you well prepared for them and know how to avoid falling victim to them. Organizations need to be constantly enlightening their employees, partners and customers as regards social engineering to reduce the risk of them falling prey to the techniques, and individuals on their own part should also ensure they learn about the techniques and how to avoid falling victim. It is unrealistic to think that everyone can become 100% safe from social engineering as humans have weaknesses like carelessness and forgetfulness; moreover even security experts sometimes get sloppy and fall for the simplest social engineering tricks. Hence, the objective is to reduce the risk of becoming victim to social engineering techniques to the barest minimum with enlightenment and awareness.

APPENDIX: QUIZ ANSWERS

QUIZ 1:

1. b; 2. a; 3. b; 4. a; 5. c.

QUIZ 2:

1. b. 2. c; 3. a; 4. a; 5. b.

QUIZ 3

1. b; 2. a; 3. b; 4. b; 5. a; 6. a; 7. b; 8. b.

QUIZ 4

1. c; 2. a; 3. b; 4. c; 5. a.

QUIZ 5

1. a; 2. c; 3. b; 4. a; 5. b.

QUIZ 6

1. b; 2. b; 3. b; 4. c; 5. a.

QUIZ 7

1. b; 2. b; 3. a; 4. c; 5. a.

QUIZ 8

1. c; 2. a; 3. c; 4. b; 5. a; 6. c.

QUIZ 9

1. a; 2. b; 3. a; 4. c; 5. b.

QUIZ 10

1. b; 2. c; 3. a; 4. c; 5. b.

QUIZ 11

1. a; 2. c; 3. a; 4. b; 5. b.

QUIZ 12:

1.   b;   2.   c;   3.   b;   4.   a;   5.   b.

GLOSSARY

Anti-malware: tools or programs used to protect against malware (malicious software) on an electronic device or network.

Baiting: a technique that involves a malicious actor using a form of enticement to lure unsuspecting victims into installing malware on their endpoint and/or network. This can be achieved by sending links or attachments, using flashy banners or physically strategically placing infected storage media.

Botnet: short for robot network. It is a group of connected computer systems, media and devices under the control of a malicious individual via malware without the infected users knowing. The botnet could be made up of PCs, tablets, mobile phones, smart watches or any device that can access the Internet.

Cash trap: a kind of device used by criminals to block ATM cash dispensing point's shutter which traps any cash dispensed while giving the unsuspecting victim the impression there was a dispense error. The cash trap resembles the shutter at the dispensing point so suspicion is usually not aroused by its presence as it is hardly noticeable. The criminal can then return when the ATM area is free, to retrieve the trap and the money.

CEO fraud: a type of scam in which an attacker pretends to be the top executive or a senior person in an organization in order to deceive employees into carrying out acts that would meet the attacker's objective. This could be used to get funds transferred to the fraudster or send confidential information to unauthorized elements that could lead to compromise of the victim organization.

Chain messages: sent using various communication media which lead victims to spread the message to others leading to an exponential increase in the spread of such messages.

Clickbait: a form of baiting which lures victims into clicking a URL by presenting something that would elicit curiosity. For example, on video sites a video thumbnail could show something that would encourage a victim to click on the video like an attractive lady or a trending event, even if this is not contained in the video, and so on.

Cyber attacks: attacks carried out against digital devices and platforms usually carried out by means of such devices and platforms. Attacks could be carried out against individuals, businesses, organizations or nation states with a wide range of motives like stealing, ideological attacks, espionage and so on.

Cyber crime: criminal acts carried out using digital devices and platforms like PCs, mobile phones, the Internet and so on. The target of cyber crime is similarly digital devices and platforms whether for the sake of causing damage, financial gain or compromising integrity, availability and/or confidentiality of data/information.

Cyber espionage: spying through information systems and electronic devices to steal confidential data. This could have business, political or military undertones; it could be carried out by business organizations (business purposes to get edge over competitors) or nation states (military or political motive).

Cyber security: the protection of electronic devices and platforms from risks and threats like attacks, damage, compromise and so on. This can be done by adoption of technology, policies, guidelines and procedures.

Cyber terrorism: this is where terrorists carry out attacks against information systems and infrastructure of their victims – the target victims can be organizations, nation states or a specific demographic. They victims are targeted based on political or ideological reasons.

Cyber warfare: a situation where a nation state or organization caries out attacks against another nation state's (considered an enemy) information systems and infrastructure via electronic media and platforms to cause disruption or even destruction as part of a military/political tactic. This is usually aimed at destabilizing the state perceived to be an enemy psychologically, economically and so on.

Demagnetization: this is a method of irreversibly erasing a hard disk using a magnetic field to destroy the disk.

Dumpster diving: this involves malicious attackers checking through garbage for sensitive data or information that was not properly discarded.

E-whoring: an individual claims to be a person willing to show off sexually explicit pictures or videos to potential victims in order to lure them to a porn site or dating site, or to blackmail victims.

Hacker: an individual that is engaged in the art of hacking. Although the tendency is to mostly use the term for malicious professionals, there are also hackers whose hacking is aimed at ensuring cyber security – ethical hackers.

Hacking: the art of gaining unauthorized access to information systems, whether devices or platforms, usually over a network. Hacking can also entail gaining unauthorized access to program codes such that a program can be manipulated to function in a way not intended by the original designer. Hacking is usually associated with negativity in that malicious individuals use it to gain unauthorized access and wreak havoc, but there also exists ethical hacking which uses hacking techniques to strengthen systems security.

Keystroke logger: also known as a keylogger is a surveillance tool used to record the keys pressed when a victim is typing without the knowledge of the victim. It could be in the form of hardware or software. The hardware is usually attached between a computing device and the keyboard, so it could be of PS/2 connector type or USB. Software keyloggers are installed on systems and they record what is typed on the keyboard, malicious attackers could use various methods to install keylogging software including malware and social engineering. Hardware keyloggers need to be installed physically, so the malicious individual needs to get physical access to do so, could be through piggy-backing or a malicious insider. Organizations may also use keylogging to monitor employees.

Malware: short for malicious software. These are programs designed to have negative consequences on information systems; whether causing the devices or platforms to malfunction, crash or allow unauthorized access to malicious attackers.

Personally identifiable information (PII): data and information that are specific to an individual which can be used for identification or access, like usernames and passwords, place of birth, date of birth, and other demographic information. These data are usually entered when filling online forms. PII is meant to be kept private and protected, for if it falls in the wrong hands there is no saying the limit of damage that can be done.

Phishing: a deceptive technique used to gain unauthorized access by directing to a point where victims will be compromised using communication channels and imitating a known genuine source.

Piggy-backing: a situation where an attacker gains unauthorized access to a restricted area by shadowing an authorized personnel, giving the impression that they are together.

Pretexting: a technique in which a malicious attacker deceives an unsuspecting victim by pretending to be someone else in a bid to gain unauthorized access to sensitive data and information.

Ransomware: a form of malware which locks owners of data from access to crucial data on their information systems, the data is held hostage with the malicious attacker promising to release the data in exchange for something like funds. However, the data are not always released once payment is made.

Scam messages: also known as advance fee fraud messages, Nigerian letter or 419 scam messages involve scammers tricking victims into sending them money in anticipation of receiving far more money in return.

Shoulder surfing: a method of stealing confidential and sensitive data (like login credentials) by using a form of surveillance or the other (the surveillance could be peeping over shoulder, using hidden camera or skimmers and so on).

Skimmer: a skimmer is a piece of hardware inserted into payment card reading devices at the area where cards are inserted and used to steal card details such that the compromised card can be cloned or used to carry out online transactions. There can also be fake ATMs used to steal the details, usually placed over the real ATM. Skimmers are installed secretly by malicious individuals at card transaction points, and may be installed along with a hidden camera used to steal PIN codes.

Smishing: a version of phishing that is SMS based – the attacker sends SMS text messages directing victims to a phishing site or any other means of getting the victims' credentials compromised.

Social engineer: an individual that engages in the act of social engineering.

Social engineering: Social engineering is a deceptive method adopted by malicious individuals to compromise information systems by taking advantage of inherent weaknesses of the systems' operators like gullibility, greed, willingness to help, curiosity, desire, fear and so on.

Spear phishing: a targeted form of phishing which is directed to a specific group of individuals that belong to a specific demographic – this could be individuals belonging to a certain industry, top executives, gender and so on.

Vishing: a form of phishing that uses voice messages to get victims compromised.

Worm: a type of malware that spreads over multiple computer systems through self-replication, usually over a network or promiscuous use (using on multiple computer systems, and especially without scanning) of storage devices like flash drives.

LIST OF REFERENCES

Chapman, S. (2009) *Consultant Uses Social Skills to trick Corporate Security* [Online]. Available from: https://www.cio.com/article/2428266/infrastructure/consultant-uses-social-skills-to-trick-corporate-security.html (Accessed: 27 October, 2017).

Christensen, B.M. (2017) *Teddy Bear Virus Hoax - jdbgmgr.exe* [Online]. Available from: http://www.hoax-slayer.net/teddy-bear-virus-hoax-jdbgmgr-exe/ (Accessed: 3 November, 2017).

Cima, R. (2015) *The Email Scam with Centuries of History* [Online]. Available from:

https://priceonomics.com/the-email-scam-with-centuries-of-history/ (Accessed: 20 October, 2017).

CNBC (2015) *Xoom says $30.8 mln transferred fraudulently to overseas accounts* [Online]. Available from: https://www.cnbc.com/2015/01/06/xoom-says-308-mln-transferred-fraudulently-to-overseas-accounts.html (Accessed: 23 October, 2017).

Collins, P. (2010) *You Must Forward This Story to Five Friends: The curious history of chain letters.* [Online]. Available from: http://www.slate.com/articles/arts/culturebox/2010/10/you_must_forward_this_story_to_five_friends.html (Accessed: 22 October, 2017).

Conheady, S. (2014) Social Engineering in IT Security: Tools, Tactics, and Techniques. McGraw Hill Education.

Encyclopedia Britannica (2015) *Trojan Horse | Greek Methodology* [Online]. Available from: https://www.britannica.com/topic/Trojan-horse (Accessed: 19 October, 2017).

Fuchs, E. (2014) *Here's the 1898 Version of Those Nigerian Email Scams* [Online]. Available from: http://www.businessinsider.com/charles-seife-writes-about-the-origin-of-the-spanish-prisoner-scam-2014-7?IR=T (Accessed: 20 October, 2017).

Goodchild, J. (2013) *A Real Dumpster Dive: Banks Tosses Personal Data, Checks, Laptops* [Online]. Available from: https://www.csoonline.com/article/2123810/identity-theft-prevention/a-real-dumpster-dive--bank-tosses-personal-data--checks--laptops.html (Accessed: 29 October, 2017).

Hern, A. (2018) WhatsApp to restrict message forwarding after India mob lynchings. *The Guardian*, [online]. Available from: https://www.theguardian.com/technology/2018/jul/20/whatsapp-to-limit-message-forwarding-after-india-mob-lynchings (Accessed: 18 September, 2018).

International Centre for Nigerian Law (2017) *Criminal Code Act-Part IV to the end* [Online]. Available from: http://www.nigeria-law.org/Criminal%20Code%20Act-Part%20VI%20%20to%20the%20end.htm (Accessed: 1 November, 2017).

Krebs on Security (2013) *The Biggest Skimmers of All: Fake ATMs* [Online]. Available from: https://krebsonsecurity.com/2013/12/the-biggest-skimmers-of-all-fake-atms/ (Accessed: 29 October, 2017).

Marks, P. (2010) *Why the Stuxnet worm is like nothing seen before* [Online]. Available from: https://www.newscientist.com/article/dn19504-why-the-stuxnet-worm-is-like-nothing-seen-before/ (Accessed: 16 October, 2017).

Munson, L. (2016) *The Spanish Prisoner: Birth of the 419 Scam* [Online]. Available from http://www.security-faqs.com/the-spanish-prisoner-birth-of-the-419-scam.html (Accessed: 20 October, 2017).

Panda Security (2012) *Katy Perry and Russell Brand Used as Bait to Spread New Facebook Worm, According to Panda Labs* [Online]. Available from: https://www.pandasecurity.com/mediacenter/press-releases/katy-perry-and-russell-brand-used-as-bait-to-spread-new-facebook-worm-according-to-pandalabs/ (Accessed: 2 November, 2017).

Rouse, M. (2017) *botnet* [Online]. Available from: http://searchsecurity.techtarget.com/definition/botnet (Accessed: 23 October, 2017).

Rouse, M. (2016) *What is cybersecurity?* [Online]. Available from: http://whatis.techtarget.com/definition/cybersecurity (Accessed: 1 August, 2017).

Social Engineering, Inc. (2017) *Vishing* [Online]. Available from: https://www.social-engineer.org/framework/attack-vectors/vishing/ (Accessed: 23 October, 2017).

Souza, F (2015) *Analyzing a Facebook Clickbait Worm* [Online]. Available from: https://blog.sucuri.net/2015/06/analyzing-a-facebook-clickbait-worm.html (Accessed: 2 November, 2017).

Ventura, C. (2017) Police arrest alleged "Nigerian Prince" email scammer in Louisiana. *USA Today*, [online]. Available from: https://www.usatoday.com/story/news/nation-now/2017/12/30/nigerian-prince-email-scammer-louisiana/992073001/ (Accessed: 18 September, 2018).

Zetter, K. (2014) *An Unprecedented look at Stuxnet, the World's first Digital Weapon* [Online]. Available from: https://www.wired.com/2014/11/countdown-to-zero-day-stuxnet/ (Accessed: 16 October, 2017).